The Clean Kitchen

A Division of The McGraw-Hill Companies

Columbus, Ohio

www.sra4kids.com

SRA/McGraw-Hill

A Division of The McGraw·Hill Companies

Send all inquiries to:
SRA/McGraw-Hill
8787 Orion Place
Columbus, OH 43240-4027

ISBN 0-07-569749-1
   3 4 5 6 7 8 9 DBH 05 04 03 02

"Quick, Jean, let's surprise Mom
and clean up the kitchen."

"Put the cream in the fridge. Quick, put the leftover beans and meat in, too."

The water streamed into the sink.
Dad and Jean scrubbed each fork
until it squeaked.

The plates gleamed. Dad and Jean beamed.

"Shhh. Jean, let's sneak away."

"Is this a dream? Whiskers, did
you clean up this kitchen?"